THE HEART OF MAN

Participant's Guide

The Fedd Agency
P.O. Box 341973
Austin, TX 78734
www.thefeddagency.com

Published by The Heart of Man, LLC.

ISBN: 978-1-943217-72-4

Printed in the United States of America
First Edition 15 14 13 10 09 / 10 9 8 7 6 5 4 3 2

CONTENTS

———

Resources and Recommended Reading

The journey of The Heart of Man that you are being invited to is not for the faint of heart. Being honest with yourself takes profound bravery, and sharing your darkness with others can be terrifying. We encourage you to be brave. Be courageous. Healing, hope, and power are waiting for you . . .

INTRODUCTION

Welcome fellow traveler!

Many of you who have seen *The Heart of Man* have been touched to the core. Perhaps it has helped you see yourself accurately for the first time—the way that God sees you. Even more importantly, you have also now discovered a more wonderful and accurate picture of God, the Father. For all of us, that experience and conviction of the depth of the Father's love may be a key to forever changing our relationship with Him.

This freedom is for us.

All of us.

But even at the beginning of this journey, we have to be intently discerning. For it is possible for truth to move us and still not free us.

Even though we've been through a compelling experience, offering us incredible hope, this new insight can get snatched away before we have a chance to internalize it. Each of us has a lens through which we see God and truth. Some lenses are more "sight-giving" than others.

If we see God through a lens of our shame, we will remain unconvinced that He is good, powerful, present, willing and utterly loving. We may hedge our bets and guard our hearts because it may all feel too good to be true. For we have been let down too many times. Too often, we bought into something that promised hope and never delivered.

Seeing God through a moralistic lens could compel you to respond to this film by jumping in with both feet, the way you would a New Year's exercise resolution.

"I must get to work on my shame."

"I need to be better at loving God."

"Now that I see how much God loves me, I need to be better at saying no to temptations."

It's a trap. A trap of your own design. And it will work even less well than the last twenty-seven self-improvement projects you put yourself through.

It would be hugely valuable for each of us to stop here and give an unhurried, honest response to these questions: "Do I come away from this film wanting to promise God I will do something more or better? Or, do I think I am buried so deep that I can't claw my way out of this hole?"

You will certainly not be alone if you answered yes to either question. But a "yes" answer can also sometimes cripple you or leave you pretending you're okay.

Then striving.

Then despairing.

Then hiding.

Then giving yourself permission to act out again.

There is another way.

This journey starts with community. Only in community can we try out such daring trust. It is time for a clumsily real but increasingly authentic community to set the table in this wild land.

"Is there anyplace I can go to

avoid your Spirit?

To be out of your sight?

If I climb to the sky, you're there . . .

If I flew on morning's wings

to the far western horizon,

You'd find me in a minute—

you're already there waiting."

— An Ancient Poetic Text of David

HOW TO USE
THIS GUIDE

———————

This guide is designed for both groups and individuals. If you are going on this journey with a group, we strongly suggest watching *The Heart of Man* together as your first meeting. Even if you have already seen the film separately, this can lay a powerful foundation for the rest of your time together.

This guide will take you through six Scenes, leading you through the film's story and, if you let it, your own. Each Scene will have five questions for you to consider and wrestle with. We encourage you to spend time answering these questions for yourself throughout the week. Try to be as honest as you can, even if you struggle to be self-disclosing. *Remember that there are many addictions beyond sexual struggles, and some are less obvious than others—this guide is designed to help bring freedom from both internal and external addictions.* When you get together as a group, read through the Scenes out loud and then answer the questions as they come—this will help remind you of the context of each question.

Authentic community is absolutely essential to begin breaking our painful, destructive patterns, so whether you are experiencing this journey individually or with a group, make sure to share with others what you are learning about yourself. We all have a deep, God-given longing for relationships where we feel safe, known, and loved. If we do not trust anyone enough to let them into our pain, we will continue hiding, alone and afraid to be known. Our temptations and struggles fester and grow in the darkness—it is only by bringing them into the light with others whom we trust that we can begin facing our pain and healing from our wounds.

This kind of community and trust takes great courage. The journey of *The Heart of Man* that you are being invited to is not for the faint of heart. Being honest with yourself takes profound bravery, and sharing your darkness with others can be terrifying. We encourage you to be brave. Be courageous. Healing, hope, and power are waiting for you.

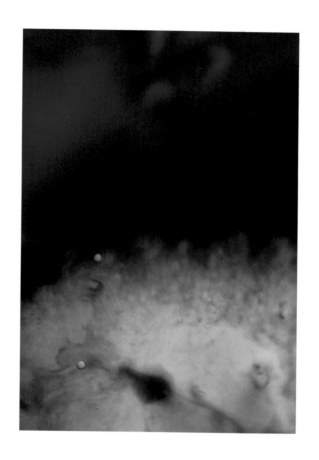

THE TABLE

*"There is a longing in the deepest parts of us to belong.
The hope that there is a table somewhere, around which we
might actually be comfortable in our own skin. We don't have
to hide. We don't have to keep our secrets. There's always been
a community of relationship. We are designed for that."*

"When I am in the Father's presence, I feel like I am at a banquet, where the table has been spread for me, and there has been such attention to detail put into every part of the meal. The true power of that meal is there is no fear in His eyes if I decide to get up and leave. Because there is always an open seat for me at His table."

—Tony Anderson

If the deepest part of us longs to belong, why do we struggle to find "a table" in most of our friendships or communities?

The Heart of Man shows us a good, trustworthy Father who stands at the head of the table, affirming, enjoying, and loving each one of us, no matter what season of life we are in. Family, friends, and newcomers to the community all sit together, some entering with others into hard places, others celebrating each other, and all enjoying a meal made with extravagant love. The depth and goodness of the relationships provide an atmosphere where pain and loss, grief and loneliness, do not carry the same power as they would in isolation. And healing is not just a theory, but an ongoing practice that takes place day in and day out.

The entire picture illustrates the care and creativity of committed friends who know they are loved, needed, and valued. Friends who know they are indispensable to each other. The strength of this community welcomes all members to come as they are, and stay as long as they like.

When you imagine sitting at the Father's table, how does it make you feel? Why?

What are the reasons we might leave the table?

An innate longing for this table, this sense of community, this place where we can be known and loved, has been woven into our very DNA! Dan Allender describes what this kind of environment, this kind of interaction with God, would be like in a shame-free world.

A SHAME–FREE WORLD

DAN ALLENDER

Try to imagine a shame-free world where there is no looking at oneself with judgment, where there is looking at the other with nothing but joy. Looking at your fellow man, your fellow woman, and your God and the world He created—all these relationships would be playful. Your day would be full—an investigation of stars, of cells, of trees. In the garden, everything would have been new and fresh and alive, and everything would have been connected to something else that one doesn't know. There would be an accumulation of joy each and every day as you climbed the highest mountains and dived the deepest oceans. At the end of your play—in the cool of the day—God shows up. And he's going to sit down with you, eager to hear what you've investigated, what you found, what kind of joy you discovered. It is sitting down with a really good brew, with a really good meal, having a conversation with a really good friend about the best things in life.

Have you ever experienced this kind of freedom and acceptance, either in your relationship with God or with others? If so, what was it like?

A community like the one Allender describes allows us to experience a Father who doesn't need us to fix ourselves up before coming into His presence.

What happened through Christ at the cross opened the door even more widely to freedom, strength, and safety with the Father. When we believe in Christ, we get to risk a life without masks, without hiding. His table is a place where you can be known deeply and don't have to worry that the Father is ever offended by the real you. In fact, He cannot wait for your next conversation! Shauna Niequist describes what is so powerful about coming to the table.

COME TO THE TABLE

"We don't come to the table to fight or to defend. We don't come to prove or to conquer, to draw lines in the sand or to stir up trouble. We come to the table because our hunger brings us there. We come with a need, with fragility, with an admission of our humanity. The table is the great equalizer, the level playing field many of us have been looking everywhere for.

The table is the place where the doing stops, the trying stops, the masks are removed, and we allow ourselves to be nourished, like children. We allow someone else to meet our need. In a world that prides people on not having needs, on going longer and faster, on going without, on powering through, the table is a place of safety and rest and humanity, where we are allowed to be as fragile as we feel."

— Shauna Niequist, *Bread and Wine*

The table is a place where there is no hiding, where we can share our brokenness with others. Some of us, tired and weary of isolation, discover we are being called by God to create such a community for ourselves and other like-hearted friends . . . maybe even someone you watched this movie with. Risking such vulnerability is the very best kind of terrifying. The alternative is staying hidden and unknown, perhaps pretending to those around you that you're doing okay even though you're in incredible pain. To feel and experience others' love, we have to trust them enough to let them into our real selves. It takes great courage, but it is worth the risk.

We noticed something else very early on at this table. Not all of us are able to fully enjoy the meal. Sometimes we're preoccupied and struggle to stay in the moment. Maybe that's how it is for you, too. Half here and half in your own head . . . islands away.

But never the Father. He is always there, and He sees what no one else can. Even while He is blessing and enjoying everyone at the table, He understands that we are islands away, and He's already planning how He will bring us back home.

This takes place at every table, in every community. Someone always hides in the midst of community, afraid to be known. The gifts of forgiveness, repentance and unconditional love are all available to everyone, at every meal. Yet our heads are elsewhere . . . lost in fantasy or intentional sin. Not even a great Father or His gracious welcome is enough to woo us away from that which remains hidden.

Have you ever been in a
safe, healthy community
and felt like you were still
hiding or were afraid to
be known?

QUESTIONS:

What did that look like for you?

What was keeping you from experiencing the moment?

FROM THE FILMMAKERS

In the opening scene, we see a character that we quickly understand is the Father in our story. He's slashing His way through a jungle, trying to get somewhere, or to something. He has a sense of determination and relentlessness. For what? We don't immediately know. This scene connects to the end of Act 2 as we again see the Father forging His way through the jungle—and it's here that we realize he is heading towards the cave where His son has been taken captive, facing destruction. This is the same path that the Father started creating at the beginning of the film —before His son had even left. He's been working on behalf of His son his entire life, to prepare the way back to unity and wholeness.

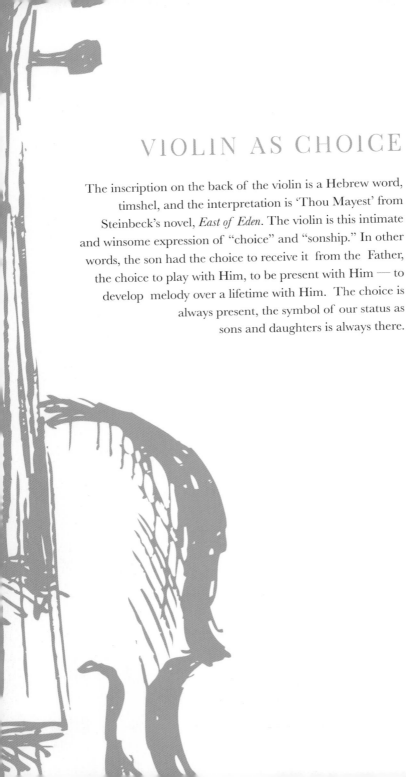

VIOLIN AS CHOICE

The inscription on the back of the violin is a Hebrew word, timshel, and the interpretation is 'Thou Mayest' from Steinbeck's novel, *East of Eden*. The violin is this intimate and winsome expression of "choice" and "sonship." In other words, the son had the choice to receive it from the Father, the choice to play with Him, to be present with Him — to develop melody over a lifetime with Him. The choice is always present, the symbol of our status as sons and daughters is always there.

THE BOAT

"We are sons and we are to call him Abba——there is something in us that knows what it is like to be so small and so protected by a great father. Most of us didn't have one, but those who did know what it is like to crawl up in his lap and have him beam over us."

*"Open your mouth and
taste, open your eyes and see—
how good God is."*
— An Ancient Poetic Text of David

—JOHN LYNCH

Often, we are confused, tripped up, even crippled by earthly fathers who were wounded by their own wounded fathers. Many of them weren't even sure they wanted to be fathers. You may have experienced firsthand being parented by a father who didn't really want to know you or be known by you. To have the person who was supposed to love you most not want to know what hurts you, or what brings you joy is devastating. To be hit, verbally or physically, by someone who knew how to parent only by fear and dominance, can handicap you. This early impression can take a lifetime to overcome.

And here's the difficult part. It is nearly impossible for a son or a daughter to not superimpose their own earthly father over their view of their heavenly Father.

"*Today I wonder why it is God refers to Himself as 'Father' at all. This, to me, in light of the earthly representation of the role, seems a marketing mistake.*"

— Donald Miller, *Blue Like Jazz*

What are some words you would use to describe your relationship with your earthly father?

If you had an earthly father in your life, how do you think he saw you while you were growing up?

PAUL YOUNG

"A lot of times our first experience of God is going to happen in any kind of a masculine sense through our relationships with our dads, or some male figure. And if that's violated, and if that person has no idea of who they are either, we still adapt to the presentation of God through that person. It took me all of fifty years to completely wipe the face of my father off the face of God."

Even the best father cannot fully and accurately express the goodness, integrity, intentionality, joyful tender-heartedness and consistency of your heavenly Father. Some fathers do present character attributes consistent with God. Oh, what a gift that is to a son or a daughter!

Yet, none of us can escape how our earthly fathers may have let us down, broken our hearts, made promises they couldn't keep, or powered up to shut us down. Many of us had fathers who never affirmed us, leaving us feeling like we weren't enough for or acceptable to him.

QUESTIONS:

How do you think your earthly father affected your view of God as the Father? If you never knew your father, how do you think your experiences with men in authority affected your view of God as the Father?

What truths do you struggle to believe about God because of this?

"*The only person who dares wake up a king at 3:00 AM for a glass of water is a child. We have that kind of access.*"

–TIMOTHY KELLER

Read Larry Crabb's description of what it means to see God as our perfect Papa, regardless of our experiences with our earthly fathers.

THE PERFECT PAPA

"Whatever your background, you and I have this in common: we all wanted, and still want, a papa. We dream of the perfect papa. We yearn for a strong man we can count on to be there for us, to want us, to look after us, to delight in us; someone we want to get close to, a lion of a man who invites us to draw near to him and rest in his powerful but gentle love.

Well, we have one. His name is God. And like the best Papa we can imagine, the sound of His footsteps, if we know who's coming, inspires exuberant joy, not cowering fear. And when we hear His voice and feel His hug, all is well. We're safe. Papa is here."

— Larry Crabb, *The Papa Prayer*

It is hard for us to believe that we have this kind of powerful, adoring, intentional Papa. Depending on your background it might be difficult to see God the Father in this intimate way. However, one of the beautiful truths of being a follower of Jesus is that God is your Father when you feel like it's true and when you don't, and you are a son or daughter when you run and hide and when you stay and enjoy His presence. Timothy Keller describes this in light of a story from a Puritan pastor.

EXPERIENCING THE FATHER

TIMOTHY KELLER

"There's an old story by Thomas Goodwin, a 17th-century Puritan pastor . . . one day Goodwin was taking a walk and saw a father and son walking along the street. Suddenly the father swept the son up into his arms and hugged him and kissed him and told the boy he loved him – and then, after a minute, he put the boy back down. Was the little boy more a son in the father's arms than he was down on the street? Objectively and legally there was no difference, but subjectively and experientially, there was all the difference in the world. In his father's arms, the boy was experiencing his sonship.

This was an assurance of who this little boy was. The love of God enables us to say to ourselves: 'If someone as all-powerful as that loves me like this, delights in me, has gone to infinite lengths to save me, says he will never let me go, and is going to glorify me and make me perfect and take everything bad out of my life—if all of that is true—why am I worried about anything? At a minimum this means joy, and a lack of fear and self-consciousness.'"

"You are the son of a kind, strong, and engaged Father, a Father wise enough to guide you in the Way, generous enough to provide for your journey, offering to walk with you every step. This is perhaps the hardest thing for us to believe—really believe, down deep in our hearts, so that it changes us forever, changes the way we approach each day."

– John Eldredge, *Fathered by God*

QUESTION:

How would your life be different if you lived convinced, deep down, that you are uniquely loved by the Maker of the entire universe?

FROM THE
FILMMAKERS

Here in the boat, we see the first moment the son is being enticed away from the presence of the Father. It's the first time, in this world, where temptation slithers in. While this is happening, we get a glimpse of the Father's face towards His son. It is not one of judgment and anger, but rather compassion and concern. We don't see the Father grab the son or forcefully pull him back. Rather, we see a Father who reminds His son, with gentleness and understanding, of all that he has access to: the fullness and richness of a relationship.

VIOLIN AS SONSHIP

To be a son or a daughter of God is something that transcends time. It means to belong to One who always pursues, always protects, always prepares, always praises our inherent worth. The experience of sonship, then, is to always be loved, cared for, attended to and esteemed. Not for what we do . . . but for who we are.

None of us have ever experienced this perfect relationship in our human families. That can mar our perception of the One who is a perfect parent, and it will always take time for that mistaken perception to be corrected.

The Father doesn't want us to try to earn our sonship because we can't. It's not about earning. It's about receiving the violin, taking it in our hands, plucking the strings, drawing back the bow, spending the time we need to learn how to experience our sonship. That is sweet music, indeed.

THE CLIFF

"Probably the most unexplainable reality in all the universe is how you can have everything and simply want something else you've been told not to get. That's madness! You've got billions of dollars and you sell your soul for a quarter that you see on the ground. Madness! Insanity! To try and explain that, all we can say is two things: God gave freedom to love and without the choice to say 'no' there's no meaning to saying 'yes.'"

"But the Hebrew word, the word timshel—'Thou mayest'— that gives a choice. It might be the most important word in the world. That says the way is open."

—John Steinbeck, East of Eden

At your own edge, what is it you believe you will gain when you jump?

And so here you are. Standing at the edge of the cliff. A cliff of your own making. And for all the arguments about the concept of free will, you always have a choice. But it doesn't always feel that way, does it? Nearly every time you've found yourself here at the precipice, you've jumped, right? That sure doesn't feel like timshel. That doesn't feel like choice. Sometimes you've even fought it for a while. But many times, even though you knew the consequences, you jumped. That's the drill we all know. Very few things in life feel as familiar as that step off the cliff.

The way back from the edge is shockingly simple. But at this place in the journey, at the brink, it's very hard to see or embrace. You aren't listening. Choice seems almost irrelevant. Perhaps you have to go over the cliff one more time before you can be shaken awake to the reality of the powerfully simple way home. Often here at the edge of the cliff we think it's only a three-foot drop – it isn't until we step off the ledge that we discover the turbulent ocean is sixty feet down. Henri Nouwen describes this moment so well in his book "The Return of the Prodigal."

LEAVING HOME

"Somehow I have become deaf to the voice that calls me the Beloved, have left the only place where I can hear that voice, and have gone off desperately hoping that I would find somewhere else what I could no longer find at home.

Leaving home is, then, much more than a historical event bound to time and place. It is a denial of the spiritual reality that I belong to God with every part of my being, that God holds me safe in an eternal embrace, that I am indeed carved in the palms of God's hands and hidden in their shadows. Leaving home is living as though I do not yet have a home and must look far and wide to find one."

— Henri Nouwen, *The Return of the Prodigal*

And so, believing we must look for a home, we find ourselves at our own cliff. Below is a description of how sin works. If you can learn this destructive cycle, you will learn how to avoid much pain from life's cliffs.

Out of the blue, something triggers your attention. A billboard, a memory, a hurtful statement, a social media comment, the wisp of an image. It doesn't have to be much. Just enough to catch your heart off-guard. Just enough to catch your eye—something seditiously attractive—enough to set the hook.

Then your self-story begins to replay itself. Your shame forms the lies and predicts the outcome. "Here we go again. Every time this hits, I will fail. Sure, I'll fight it for a moment or two. Or maybe even a long while. But in the end, I will lose. Every time."

QUESTION:

Is there anything you are carrying right now that could send you off a cliff?

Then the temptation hits. A real opportunity. A choice to actively do something wrong. It's no longer just a vague potential in your head. Here comes the whisper inside you: "You know you want it. You deserve it. You have not been treated well by God or the significant others in your life. And God does not seem to be able to help you with this stuff anyway. Just say 'yes,' and the gears will get rolling. You don't even have to admit to yourself that you made the choice. Just say 'yes.'"

Now the crime is set in motion. There is an actual place and time or perhaps even a person.

Next, you resist. Pitifully, this is the most laughable part of the story. You actually think you can fight it. Well, part of you does anyway. Here's the insanity of this part of the transaction. You are trying to fight the sin you've already given yourself permission to carry out. And the longer you fight it, the more the anticipated pleasure of the event increases. What a trap.

Unless and until this comes to the light, you will always, inevitably, invariably lose. You will act out. Period.

"Eventually, we realize, it's an addiction . . .

it's going to kill us."

—DAN ALLENDER

―――――――――

"The secret became enormous. It became suffocating. It became a slippery slope that nothing is sacred because when the pain is to a point, it's whatever it takes to get that next fix. That became my existence. The shame of my inability to say no."

‒TRAYLOR LOVVORN

―――――――――

QUESTION:

Is there anyone you trust enough to tell what you are wrestling with right now?

If you have chosen not to disclose where you are, you will step off the cliff. Yet even then, the Father is not done. He has not washed His hands of this, or you. He never will. Henri Nouwen continues the story in *The Return of the Prodigal* below, reminding us that God is never done.

ON YOU MY FAVOR RESTS

"God has never pulled back his arms, never withheld his blessing, never stopped considering his son the Beloved One. But the Father couldn't compel his son to stay home. He couldn't force his love on the Beloved. He had to let him go in freedom, even though he knew the pain it would cause both his son and himself. It was love itself that prevented him from keeping his son home at all cost. It was love itself that allowed him to let his son find his own life, even with the risk of losing it.

Here the mystery of life is unveiled. I am loved so much that I am left free to leave home. The blessing is there from the beginning. I have left it and keep on leaving it. But the Father is always looking for me with outstretched arms to receive me back and whisper again in my ear: 'You are my Beloved, on you my favor rests.'"

– Henri Nouwen, *The Return of the Prodigal*

Even here at the cliff, even though you are free to leave home, the Father is calling you "Beloved." He has given you "timshel," a true and real choice. But will-power and white-knuckled resistance have nothing to do with choice. They are a feeble coping mechanism.

Timshel is actually the choice to trust others with you or to trust yourself with you. That's the choice. And first in the "others" line is always the Father. Will you trust who the Father says He is, and who He says you are? Will you trust what the Father has done? At some point you will have to bet everything on His ability to show you a new way, to make you clean. You will have to trust that He carries no anger, resentment or disgust and will never wave a list of grievances in front of you. You must believe that His unconditional love towards you will never, ever fail or change.

Next, you will have to trust that there is at least one other person in your life who can hear your intention and not run from you. He or she will be a person prepared by the Father, that you must be willing to tell what you are intending to do.

"What if there were a place so safe that the worst of me could be known, and I would discover that I would be loved more in the telling of it, not less?"

—BO'S CAFE, JOHN LYNCH, BRUCE MCNICOL, BILL THRALL

If you would, picture yourself stepping back from your cliff for just a moment, far enough so that you can take a deep breath and let this question wash over you.

Do you believe that telling another person about the sin you are tempted by could actually stop it in its tracks? Why or why not?

FROM THE FILMMAKERS

Here is the climax of Act 1, the moment that the son's choices have led him to—the edge of the cliff. While he is walking toward his demise, what is the Father doing? What is His face saying in that moment? He's continuing to play their song on his violin, continuing to remind the son, through their shared melody, what he has access to.

VIOLIN AS HARMONY

We all understand that feeling when the music stops or ends in a relationship. Because words have wounded us. Because attention has been directed elsewhere. Because neglect has become the norm. Because a secret has been exposed . . . or because ours remain hidden.

This is a big loss when we see that the word harmony comes from a Greek root meaning "to fit together." We were meant for harmony with each other; we were created "to fit together" with the Creator who formed us in His image and to make beautiful music in unison. It is said in music that harmony is the "vertical" aspect of music—it is also the vertical aspect of relationship.

The heart of man is this: We are made for harmony with the heart of God, even if it becomes a broken harmony that needs restoration. And that can happen if we will only dare to believe it.

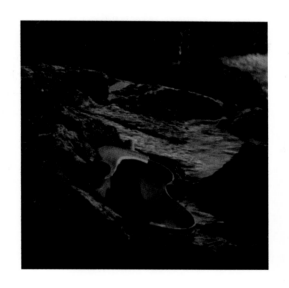

THE LAGOON

"Here in the lagoon, your fantasy is shown to be what it was all along—death wrapped in a prettier package. The lagoon is that cruel moment when not only your failure and wounds have been revealed, but when you discover you sacrificed so much to gain hideousness that will not readily go away."

"I darted with all the force of swimming I had to where she was, and then nearly fainted, for she was old and hideous and her feet were deformed and turned inwards and her skin was wrinkled and, worst of all, she was a leper. You have never seen a leper, I suppose; until you have seen one you do not know the worst that human ugliness can be. This creature grinned at me, showing a toothless mask, and the next thing I knew, I was swimming along in my old way in the middle of the stream—yet trembling."

— Malcolm Muggeridge, *Letter to His Father*

QUESTION:

What lies does your shame tell you when you wade into your lagoon?

When any of us choose to step off the cliff and end up in the lagoon, there are consequences—to us, and those closest to us. Their story of discovering that we stepped off the cliff is often more painful than even our story of hiding, acting out, and the shame from our actions.

QUESTIONS:

Is God with you in the lagoon? How would anything change if you knew He is actually with you in these moments, loving you?

What is God's expression when your sins are exposed here in the lagoon (remember, the lagoon is not always about sexual sin)?

BROKEN

JULIANNE CUSICK

"When we were engaged, or dating before we were engaged, he said, "You know, I need to tell you about my history. I've struggled with sex addiction and pornography and these are the ways I've acted out…" and I said, "Well, okay, but I won't tolerate any of that in our marriage."

God, so naïve.

So here we are, married for three years, and Michael would say, 'I love you,' but I would feel hated. I remember that. We would have a supposedly romantic dinner, and I remember he gave me a gift and said all these words and I remember thinking, 'This is such a crock of shit. I don't feel any of this and I don't think you do either.'

It was shortly after that, not even two weeks after, where he was working on this on-call job, when he called me. Apparently, he had had a call, he was out at the hospital and he said, 'Well I'm waiting for another call to come in.' Twenty minutes later he walks in the door and I said, 'Uh, what are you doing home?' He said, 'Well I was finished.' I said, 'No, you didn't say you were finished. You said you were waiting for another call—you thought another call was going to come in.'

The blood drained out of his face. 'Well I thought it was coming . . . or it ended up . . . they called and they didn't need me . . .' blah, blah, bullshit. Then he said the words that every woman dreads: 'There's something I need to tell you.'

I knew it was bad. He was white as a ghost and inside my stomach and heart plummeted. I don't even remember what he started to tell me at that point, but over the next three days he shared every incident of drinking at lunch or taking prostitutes to lunch and going to adult bookstores, massage parlors, or strip clubs, or video arcades to watch porn. Everything that I had known and believed in was just gone—decimated. The first night I locked my bedroom door and fell asleep to him crying in the other room. The only gift he gave me in the midst of such tragedy was his brokenness at how he had broken me. That response was a gift. He didn't minimize it. He didn't gloss over it. He was devastated by how much pain I was in and what he had done.

My entire life changed that day. I had changed that day. We went to counseling and I said, 'I feel hated. He says he loves me but I feel hated.'

At one point he said, 'I do hate you.' And I thought, Amen. Praise God. What a relief, thank you. That's the truth. Now we can go somewhere. I would rather be hurt by the truth than be comforted with a lie. That was where our marriage really began to fall apart—when everything was broken.

Our marriage falling apart, our marriage being dismantled, my brokenness being exposed, was the greatest gift we ever received in our marriage because it literally gave us the opportunity to have a marriage."

"Then there is the
self-repulsion. This is the
self-awareness painted by my
shame. No matter what you did
to try and clean yourself up, to
look good, to play the right part,
to say the right things, shame was
always there to tell you you're
not. You're a joke. You're a fool,
look at you. You're bad. And
when you're bad, God doesn't love
you—He wants nothing to do with
you. You have to earn that love."

—KEVIN TRIPLETT

"I was always afraid that my addiction had disqualified me from any kind of relationship with God. And I can't tell you how many times I told him, I'm done. I've felt enough guilt, enough shame and I'm going to be clean from here on out. So I worked—hard—to get back into the Father's love. And to any kind of place to where I felt relationally good."

—TONY ANDERSON

This self-repulsion, this awareness of what you have done, usually leads to self-rescue. You put all your effort into making up for what you've done, into cleaning yourself up, into getting "back to the Father."

QUESTION:

The lagoon is the "failure place" where we all make promises to God. Can you describe what your "lagoon promises" to God have been? How do you try to earn your way back into His favor?

SHAME ISN'T GOING TO DO IT

"Shame does not lead us to God. It actually drives us further away from His kind, merciful, and good heart. Shame is not a sign of repentance, nor will it usher in the growth we long for. We do become even more ourselves as we repent of areas in our lives that have nothing to do with faith or love, but God does not live in a perpetual state of disappointment over who we are. Berating ourselves for our flaws and our weakness only serves to undermine our strength to become.

Repenting from our sin is essential. Beating ourselves up for sinning is no longer an option . . . God invites us to join Him in the process whereby He heals our inner world so he can transform our outer world. The process of deep, from-the-heart healing, growth, transformation, and freedom begins when we believe we are loved."

– Stasi Eldridge, *Free to Be Me*

Your lagoon experience will always be messy. It will never resolve without pain and scars. And making sincere promises won't mitigate the consequences of bad choices.

Repentance becomes the most beautiful word you can find. But this repentance cannot be one that requires more self-effort or one that beats you up.

Repentance isn't doing something about our sin; it is admitting that we can't do anything about our sin.

True repentance is fully dependent upon God. It means trusting in His complete power to erase your shame and self-disgust. It is tapping into the greatest power in the universe and believing that this power can cleanse you of the heinous result of your choices, redeem you and give you power to no longer stay here. It is powerful enough to break the spell of this madness.

QUESTION:

What might occur if you believed God wanted to help you carry this burden and that it could be this all-encompassing and immediate?

If you try to clean yourself up, if you think your sobriety for a few days or weeks will pave your own way back into the Father's presence, there's another place you will inevitably take yourself.

It is called the cave.

"Repentance, whenever you find yourself doing it, is always a gift."

–AN ANCIENT
LETTER OF PAUL,
PARAPHRASED

FROM THE FILMMAKERS

As the prodigal is about to enter the jungle in pursuit of the siren character, we see him briefly turn around. It's because he hears the melody of the Father, who is still playing on the edge of the cliff—wooing His son back home, reminding him of all that he has access to—the community and the bounty of the family table.

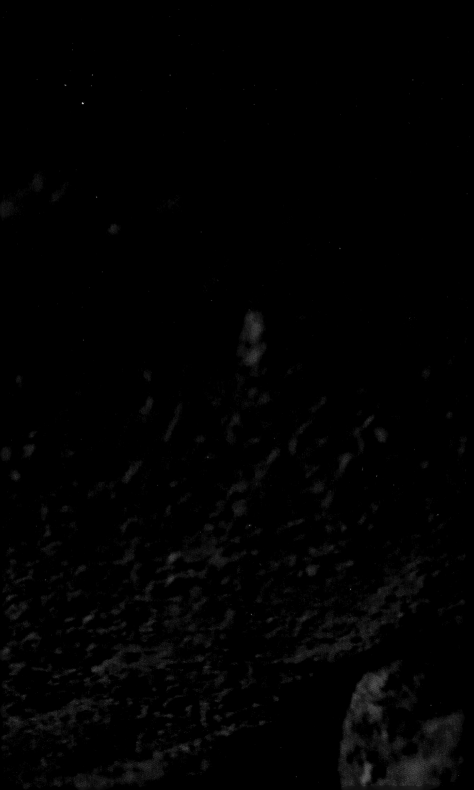

Scene 5

THE CAVE

"I wonder if one of the greatest truths that I and people like me might hear is that God is with me in my darkness. That God is with me in my shame. And that He's with me in my addiction, in my pain, in my unsettledness, in my woundedness that I don't want anybody else to see."

"There is a character in the story that hates goodness and beauty and truth. And that character despises the beauty of God."

—Dan Allender

> *"When the prodigal hits the bottom,*
> *something can grow."*
>
> —PAUL YOUNG

We have come to what seems like the end of the road—the cave. Alone, enslaved, ashamed and often believing that you are too far gone for help. You can stay here. You have stayed here. Wallowing in self-pity, eventually no longer being beaten up, but beating yourself up. Nobody can hurt you like you.

There is an evil one who has waited for you to arrive at the cave, who wants to destroy you. It is his voice you've been listening to all along. And now you see it. You are being torn apart by the one who whispered the goodness of this seditious choice. You have been seduced by a creature more deceptive, more vulgar and hideous than the sin he enticed you into. Yet the Father has already planned how He will use this pain to bring healing and redemption to your life, as Jay Stringer describes.

AN UNCANNY MAP

"Unwanted sexual behavior, be that pornography, an affair, buying sex, and the like reveal far more than just your sin. It reveals the un-examined and therefore unresolved issues of your life. Sexual behavior serves as an uncanny map. It displays the locations of our past harm and the present-day roadblocks we do not know how to navigate.

We are more likely to be ashamed of our sexual struggles when we do not understand them. It is key for us to understand that our behaviors are never random or capricious. There is always a reason. If you want freedom, you must identify the unique reasons that brought you here.

Fortunately, God is not ashamed of your sexual struggles. He under-stands them to be the very stage through which the work of redemption could be played out in your life. Most of us, however, look at our sexual failures with self-hatred. We despise ourselves for returning to a behavior that consistently hemorrhages our soul with shame. The tragedy is that this self-contempt is the very thing that blinds us from seeing the kind heart of the Father.

Sexual failure is the geography of the arrival of God. The presence of God is most often found in places of human weakness and struggle throughout the scriptures. Why would it be any other way for us? The Father enters the cave of our shame, not to condemn us, but to open our hearts to hear the music of redemption. He intends to heal your sexual struggles, but He is not content to stop there. Present sin is always the doorway to the wider work of the gospel. The gospel brings healing to the wounds of the past, and comfort, even power to the difficulties of the present. May we turn from our self-hatred to receive the kind and curious face of God."

– Jay Stringer

The cave is the final destination on the road to the evil one's ultimate sleight of hand—a believable lie. It's a lie that says this time you have gone too far. "I am unlovable. God must condemn my filth and degradation. I am too broken, too failed, too disgusting to love. Not just that big love He has for the whole universe. That love doesn't really help me right here. It's too general. I need to know that He loves me. Uniquely and distinctly me. Here, in all the moments of my betrayal.

I know He died on the cross. I know that gets me to heaven. But this . . . this stuff I do—that's different. It feels too ugly, too repeated, too indifferent to the holiness of God. Could it be true . . . that even this is covered by Jesus?"

The moment you put your faith in what Jesus did on the cross for you, all manner of incredible happens to you. Near the top of the astonishing list of realities is this: You receive a brand new core identity. Your shame story, all of it, was eradicated at the cross. When your name is brought up in heaven, no one sees you identified in your shame. They see an endlessly more outstanding you. They see Christ in you.

You might think, "That must be a misprint. It can't be as easy that that."

It isn't. And it wasn't, that day on the cross. What Jesus accomplished allowed the most scandalous approach to be His plan. He would be able to meet you in your shame, in your fear, failure, self-hatred, and loss of hope. And you are made righteous, made holy, called holy. You were never a saved sinner. You are a saint, who yes, messes up. A brand new shame-free creature.

QUESTION:

*What difference would it make for you to believe
that God is with you in the darkness?*

TONY ANDERSON

"When I choose to run from Him, into the darkness, He's
with me in that moment. And He's not angry. And His fa-
cial expression is fixed on mine, and He's loving me. And
He wasn't demanding that I stop—He was demanding
that I invite Him into that moment, to help me understand
how I got into that moment, and what's beneath that moment, and to help me search for what I'm really searching
for. Man, I melted. You know it's one thing to read, "I'm
loved." It's one thing to read, "I'll be with you." But for
Him to be with me in my addiction, for Him to be with me
in prison, and in sickness, and in relapse over and over and
over again, that's what changes me."

086

When the Father enters the cave, He goes to His son with incredible gentleness and tenderness. He doesn't demand for the son to get up or clean himself off. He holds him, and comforts him, and invites him to play the violin again. How would your life be different if you believed that God the Father saw you and treated you that way?

You have a choice to continue in the lie you have been buying. If you see yourself as a saved sinner, you will always believe you are a disappointment to the Father. If you trust your assessment of yourself, you will act out of that. You'll never be enough, and you will give yourself permission to fail over and over. Because that's what someone like you does. You have to hide. You have to pretend. You have to wear masks. And, it gets stronger and worse and more intense. It costs the people around you.

Or you can make a different choice, for moments at a time at first, to trust who God says you are. You are new. You are righteous. You are already forgiven. You are His beloved. And inside you dwells rightness, holiness, cleanliness, power, and beauty. Jesus did this. Jesus did all that re-wiring in you the day you trusted Him on the cross.

That's the choice you have before you. It's scary to truly believe it. It's hard to trust it could be true. It's hard for you to dare risk it because you see your own behavior, so you have to no longer trust your assessment of yourself and instead make this incredible daring gamble that He's right. That God's right. That this is who you are.

———

"But when we tap into God's opinion—and it's an absolute opinion,

it's an opinion that has authority and holds weight in eternity—

when we tap into that, we've tapped into what makes us, us. We've

tapped into what makes us human."

–JACKIE HILL PERRY

———

If you believed that you received a shame-free identity the moment you put your hope in Jesus, what difference would it make? Even now, after your most recent failure?

If you have not put your hope and trust in Jesus, what could be your next step?

Many of us picture Jesus "over there," on the other side of our sin. Trueface discusses why this is no longer true for followers of Jesus.

NEVER ON THE OTHER SIDE

TRUEFACE

"For many of us, our memory is rooted in being really close to Jesus when we first came to know Him. Really close. Like we could touch Him. And then over time, our failures created this mound of stuff and junk—all the stuff that a first-century man named Paul says, 'The things I said I wouldn't do I did. The things I said I would do I didn't.'

These failures formed a hill of hot steamy mess, and it seemed like Jesus went over on the other side of that mound, getting further and further away from us. But the reality is that Jesus adores us and He has never, for those that have put their hope in Him, been on the other side.

There was an ancient prophet named Jeremiah who said, 'The heart is deceitful above all things and beyond cure. Who can trust it?' It can't be trusted. It's evil. It is full of wickedness. And you will hear this concept preached often, and we end up believing this message. But, Jesus is the cure. And, He actually gave us a new heart. A new heart which can be trusted.

Another prophet named Ezekiel came after Jeremiah and heard God say to us, 'I will give you a new heart and put a new spirit in you; I will remove from you your heart of stone and give you a heart of flesh.' We start from that place of a 'new heart,' a shame-free heart, and go forward with our failure. This makes all the difference!

Jesus is saying that Jeremiah was right, but that his words are no longer true of followers of Jesus. 'Believer, that's no longer who you are. You are now delightful. At the core is this beautifully-made person who is actually righteous. Your heart can be trusted.' We're not just talking about being righteous forensically or judicially, but we carry all the righteousness of Jesus. We carry all His holiness. Otherwise, He could not even live in us. This is the miracle Jesus Christ performed for us!"

QUESTION:

If you know Jesus, what difference does it make that He is not on the other side of your sin?

"God wants you naked. Why? Because He wants to clothe you. God wants to enter into your heartache. Why? Because He really wants to bring you a taste of joy. So often we think God is just trying to get us to conform when really He's committed to unbelievable transformation. If we could only enter the depths of His love, we would find our lives deeply changed."

—DAN ALLENDER

How can the community you are part of learn to talk honestly and openly about the issues that can drive us into hiddenness?

"He has come to set us free—to be fully human and fully alive."

– PAUL YOUNG

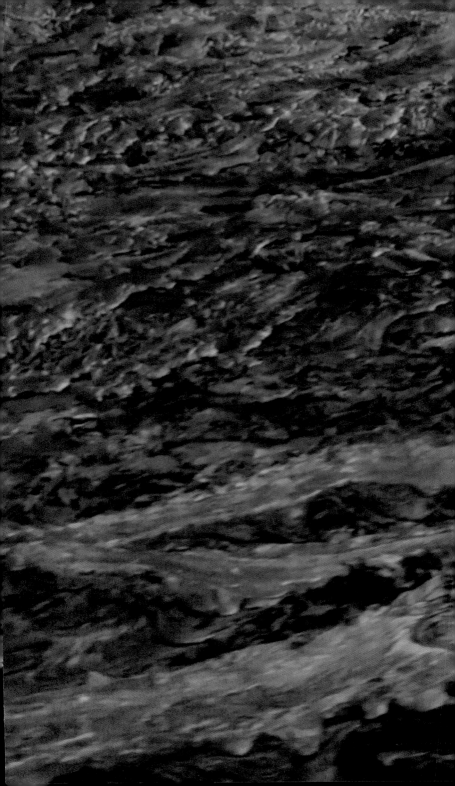

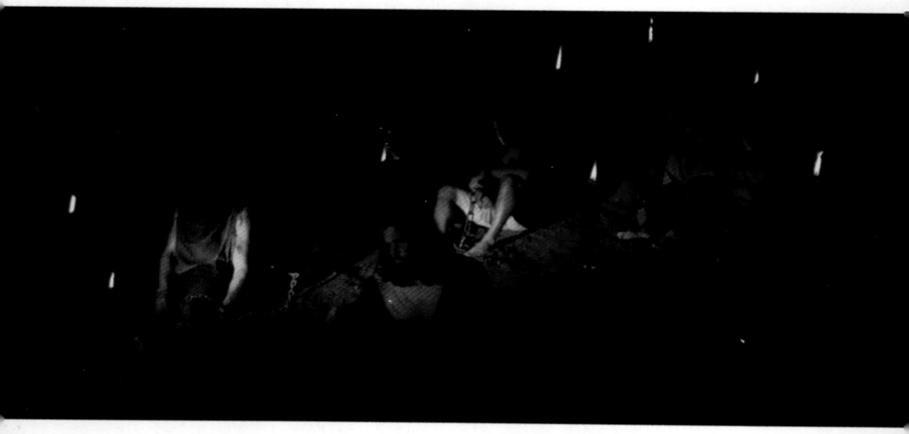

FROM THE
FILMMAKERS

There's a moment after the Father and son get up in the cave, where the back of the cave is revealed for the first time and it's full of other people. We see a glimpse into the greater cave reality—the corners are filled with others who've been shackled there by shame. And because shame isolates, you think you are alone. You don't even notice you are surrounded by fellow prisoners. You think that the shackles are unique to you, that no one else would understand. The reality is, we've all been shackled in the cave.

Many viewers ask us, did the Father and Prodigal help the other prisoners when they left the cave? We see them walk toward the others, but we didn't include what happens next because there are mysteries and questions we'll never have answered. Some choose the freedom offered by the Father, but some choose to stay shackled. The big idea here is that there are always others in our caves and that the only way out is through authentic community.

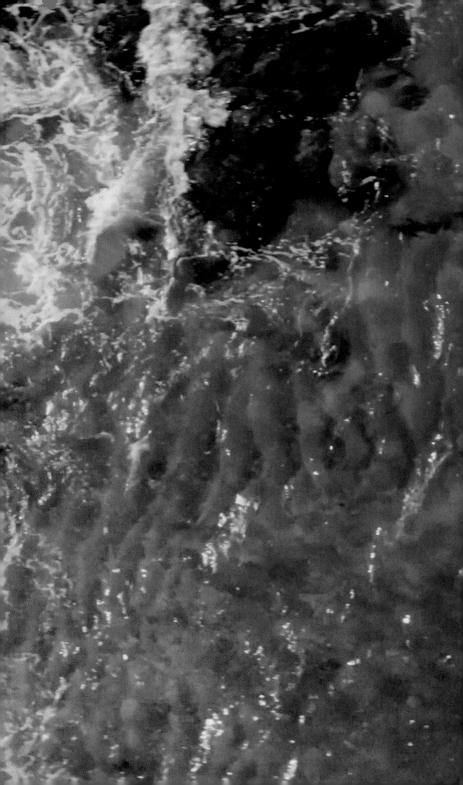

WEEK 6

THE FEAST

"He is the perpetual wave against the rocks and He is relentless in His pursuit of my heart. He sees things in me that I barely know myself. Good things. Real things. Things that are alive. And I'm starting to see that He didn't just die for my sin. He died to free me from the shame that used to define my life. I'm starting to believe that He is a good father. And that I am a good son."

The feast you're invited to does not begin when you sit down at the table. The feast begins with intimacy and time alone with the Father—fishing, talking, even laughing as you prepare for a meal together. The Father continues to invest in your relationship together, in work and play and everything in between. Together you arrive at the table, with fish to share and stories to tell.

Read an excerpt from *The Cure* below about what this community can look like.

SINGING SONGS AND TELLING STORIES

"To give love that can be trusted is the end goal of receiving love. This is where life gets worth living. It jump-starts one of the most profoundly beautiful and miraculous chain reactions anyone gets to witness in this lifetime. Closed, broken, bluffing men and women come squinting out of dark corners and into the light, singing songs and telling stories they didn't know were in them. They begin to feel alive, secure in His embrace, seeing the world for the first time in full color. Each becomes real, safe, creative, and unimpeachable. Almost involuntarily, they begin to offer to all around them a love as rich and freeing as what they are taking in.

Slowly, almost imperceptibly, that miraculous world where we were best known returns, only now even more beautiful. Hurt is transformed into relationships of trusted love. There is unspoken permission for others to tell hard truth, even clumsily expressed.

By day, we work and play hard. At night we lie on our backs in fields, talking unhurriedly about everything and anything. There we have our best conversations about God. There is little posturing, bluffing, hiding, pretending, or deceiving. Few care about who is more talented or better looking. This is the stunning power of love. This is what Jesus came for us to realize. It is not an illusion or a nostalgic childhood memory. It is ours for the taking."

– John Lynch, Bruce McNicol, and Bill Thrall, *The Cure*

QUESTION:

How does it feel to be back at the table after you have chosen to be away for awhile?

Those closest to the Father are those who are in touch with a desire for which there is no full satisfaction in this present world. Ironically, they turn out to be the ones who can best taste flavors of the feast and enjoy the simplest of meals. C.S. Lewis reminds us that these desires should draw us toward our true home.

DESIRE FOR OUR TRUE COUNTRY

"Creatures are not born with desires unless satisfaction for those desires exists. A baby feels hunger: well, there is such a thing as food. A duckling wants to swim: well, there is such a thing as water. Men feel sexual desire: well, there is such a thing as sex. If I find in myself a desire, which no experience in this world can satisfy, the most probable explanation is that I was made for another world. If none of my earthly pleasures satisfy it, that does not prove that the universe is a fraud. Probably earthly pleasures were never meant to satisfy it, but only to arouse it, to suggest the real thing. If that is so, I must take care, on the one hand, never to despise, or to be unthankful for, these earthly blessings, and on the other, never to mistake them for the something else of which they are only a kind of copy, or echo, or mirage. I must keep alive in myself the desire for my true country, which I shall not find till after death; I must never let it get snowed under or turned aside; I must make it the main object of life to press on to that country and to help others to do the same."

— C.S. Lewis, *Mere Christianity*

What difference would it make to discover there is nothing in this world that will fully satisfy this ache and longing inside of us?

You will never become less or more of Christ in you. And today, after your worst failure, you are as fully loved, adored and righteous as the first moment you believed. When you find yourself risking to trust this way of seeing, the power of the lie begins to fade and the increasing confidence of who you really are becomes the bedrock that will break your shame and addiction. It will allow you to live free.

And it turns out that the community you left is the very thing that beckons you to return and stay. What a marvelous answer and gift from the hand of the Father that those across the table and next to you are your protection, not your escape, from what you fear the most.

"There's more wholeness—and yet the paradox—I'm more broken than I've ever been."

–DAN ALLENDER

What if it were possible that you've been missing the most satisfying parts of life because you've been preoccupied with imposters of satisfaction? What hope would this bring to you?

"And so though I may be tempted, my temptations don't govern who I am, what Christ did on the cross for me does. And so when I see the temptation to lust after somebody, I'm not governed by that."

–JACKIE HILL PERRY

It is important to know that you will arrive at the cliff again. Christ tells us that we will face many trials and temptations in this world, and inevitably you will find yourself standing on the edge of your cliff again. The Father will be playing His melody for you, inviting you as you venture near the edge into a choice of trust. Which story will you believe? Are you a failure who must jump, because that's what someone like you does? Or are you a beloved child, free from shame, and free to invite others into your cliff moment? Free to stay?

Do you believe that you are a failure who must jump or a beloved child who is free from shame?

How does this change your cliff moments?

Talk to the Father, and give yourself time to listen. What is His expression when He looks at you at the feast? Who does He say you are?

"Who you are matters and who you are becoming matters. And the truth of who you are matters. You're the one that He left the ninety-nine to go find. You matter."

–PAUL YOUNG

FROM THE FILMMAKERS

Toward the end of the film, we see the son back at the table with the Father and others in his community, but something is different. His face now bears the scars of his choices. That's the reality, the earthly consequences of timshel. We might be back in relationship with the Father and others, but our war wounds from life, this side of eternity, have impact on both ourselves and those around us. Our choices will have good and bad outcomes.

That table is set with the feast once again and it's a feast with people that know the son—fully. The good, bad and ugly. He's in a community, after all of his bad decisions, where he's known fully at his worst and loved all the more. The Father's incredible love and this community will be the saving grace for him all the days of his life.

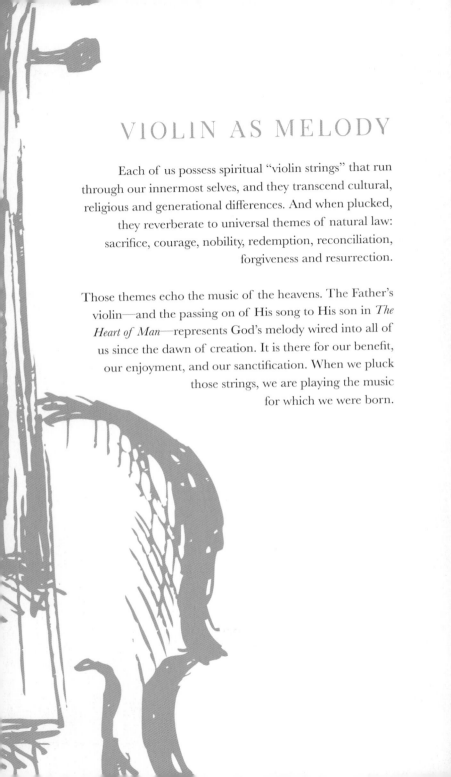

VIOLIN AS MELODY

Each of us possess spiritual "violin strings" that run through our innermost selves, and they transcend cultural, religious and generational differences. And when plucked, they reverberate to universal themes of natural law: sacrifice, courage, nobility, redemption, reconciliation, forgiveness and resurrection.

Those themes echo the music of the heavens. The Father's violin—and the passing on of His song to His son in *The Heart of Man*—represents God's melody wired into all of us since the dawn of creation. It is there for our benefit, our enjoyment, and our sanctification. When we pluck those strings, we are playing the music for which we were born.

THE HOPE

Resources To Help After Your Six-Scene Journey

Healing and recovery is not an event. It is a journey, a process. What took years to accumulate will not be undone in a beautiful film or a powerful six weeks. But there is much hope ahead. Below are some of the rich resources which can help you along your path. The most important part of the path is to have at least one other traveling with you— better still two, and even better a group.

Additional authors, organizations, counselors and other resources can be found at www.HeartofManMovie.com

RESOURCES FROM
THIS GUIDE:

The Allender Center
at The Seattle School

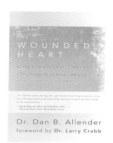

The Wounded Heart, Dan Allender
www.theallendercenter.org

*"The work of restoration cannot
begin until a problem is fully faced."*

PAUL YOUNG

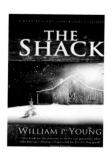

*"I suppose that since most of our
hurts come through relationships
so will our healing."*

TRUEFACE

The Cure, John Lynch,
Bill Thrall, Bruce McNicol
www.trueface.org

*"What if God wasn't on the
other side of our sin?"*

The Cure & Parents, John Lynch,
Bruce McNicol, Bill Thrall
www.trueface.org

*"It's less important that anything
gets fixed than that nothing
has to be hidden."*

LARRY CRABB

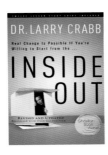

*"Change from the inside out
involves a steadfast gaze upon our
Lord that's life changing because
it reflects a deep turning from a
commitment to self-sufficiency. "*

HENRI NOUWEN

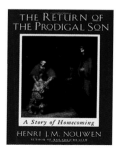

"The question is not "How am I to love God?" but "How am I to let myself be loved by God?" God is looking into the distance for me, trying to find me, and longing to bring me home."

TIMOTHY KELLER

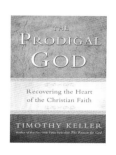

"God's reckless grace is our greatest hope, a life-changing experience, and the subject of this book."

www.purehope.net

"God's story of sex is an altogether different kind of story—one full of identity, meaning, joy, healing, and love. Written into your very nature. Etched into eternity."

REFERENCED IN THIS GUIDE

Dan Allender, The Allender Center
Tony Anderson, Tony Anderson Music
Larry Crabb, *The Papa Prayer*
Michael and Julianne Cusick, *Restoring the Soul*
John and Stasi Eldredge, *Ransomed Heart*
Timothy Keller, Redeemer Presbyterian Church
Traylor Lavvorn, *Undone Redone*
C.S. Lewis, *Mere Christianity*
John Lynch, Trueface
Donald Miller, *Blue Like Jazz*
Malcolm Muggeridge, *Letter to His Father*
Shauna Niequist, *Bread and Wine*
Henri Nouwen, T*he Return of the Prodigal*
Jackie Hill Perry, www.JackieHillPerry.com
John Steinbeck, *East of Eden*
Jay Stringer, The Allender Center
Kay Warren, Saddleback Church
Paul Young, *The Shack*

CONTRIBUTORS TO THIS GUIDE

Brian Bird, Believe Pictures
Noel Bouché, pureHOPE
The Fedd Agency
Jens Jacob, Sypher Studios
Bruce McNicol, Trueface
Rex Minor, Smokey Hill Vineyard Church
Jason Pamer, Sypher Studios
Brittany Sawrey, Trueface
Brad Smith, Bakke Graduate University
David Pinkerton, Trueface

OUR BROKENNESS

IS A BRIDGE,

NOT A BARRIER.

THE HEART OF MAN